# THE RESURRECTION, HOW EVERYTHING CHANGED

## Tom Molnar

*Apple Valley Press*

*The Resurrection, How Everything Changed*

Copyright © 2015

Apple Valley Press

ISBN 978-0-9766952-3-3

*Other Books by Tom Molnar*

Nonfiction

A Quick Look at Heaven

Mary, the Girl who said Yes.

Christianity, the Challenge of a Changing World

Fiction

Dark Age Maiden

Tara's World

Love Stories from the Heart

*All available on Amazon*

Thank you to all those who have reviewed this book. Your suggestions have helped to make this final edition better and more complete.

# Contents

# Introduction

There are many resurrection accounts. Though similar, there are significant differences recorded even in the gospels of Matthew, Mark, Luke and John.

In taking a close look at what actually happened, this account notes the differences, but does not attempt to explain them away. Instead it presents a realistic picture of Jesus and his followers after the resurrection. It illustrates a major change in Christ's objectives, and shows how the coming of the Holy Spirit transformed the lives of the apostles and his followers down to the present age.

Many are aware that the teachings of the man who was crucified spread rapidly from Palestine to Greece, to Rome and from there throughout most of the then known world. The tradition of Christianity continues into our own time, for reasons that at first glance may seem inexplicable. However, the raw power of the religion, and the ardent feelings of many, continue to excite followers and draw others into its churches. Despite this, some in the modern age find its beliefs untenable. This is related to a currently popular perception of the world, which will later be considered.

Almost 2000 years ago a holy man died. He died in a most horrible manner, on a cross, an instrument of torture devised by Persians hundreds of years before Christ and used extensively by the Romans. We have most of his message as recorded in the gospels. Non-biblical accounts also chronicle his death. Christians believe he rose from the dead. What happened after the resurrection shows that not only was the man changed, but the scope of his message changed as well. The man, Christ, is the leader of the largest religious community in the world. We call ourselves Christians.

# Chapter One
## Those who answered His call

They could not grasp the cross. Christ told his apostles several times that his death was coming and that he would rise again. To cite one example from Mark: "He began to teach them that the Son of Man must suffer greatly and be rejected by the elders, the chief priests, and the scribes, and be killed, and rise after three days." (Mark 8: 31)

Somehow, Christ's words didn't seem to sink into their heads. Christ's followers were diverse. One, Simon, was a member of the Zealot party, who sought to overthrow the Roman occupation. Years later, in 66AD, the Zealots did take up arms against the Romans. Unfortunately, this resulted in the complete destruction of the temple and the city of Jerusalem. Another of Christ's apostles was Matthew, who was a tax collector. He collected taxes for the Romans, and thus was hated by the Jews. Either Matthew himself, or one of his followers wrote the Gospel of Matthew. Women also followed Christ, though perhaps not in all his journeys. Luke's gospel names them.

"Accompanying him went the Twelve, as well as certain women who had been cured of evil spirits and ailments. Mary, surnamed the Magdalene, from whom seven demons had gone out, Joanna, the wife of Herod's steward, Chuza, Susanna and many others who provided for them out of their own resources." (Luke 8: 1-3) As can be seen, a variety of people followed Christ, some well off and others of ordinary means. Probably no other leader could unite such a disparate group. They followed a man whose message and manner resonated in their hearts.

As for the men, what kind of men did Jesus choose to be his apostles? As many as half or more were fishermen. Not poor anglers as you might imagine, standing with fishing poles on the shoreline. These men owned sizeable boats and their livelihood depended on large catches. The Sea of Galilee then and today provides fish not only for the towns around the lake but also for Jerusalem, Damascus and even Rome. Fish not sold locally had to be dried, salted and shipped. A small industry existed in Magdala where fishermen brought their catch to be sold to those who salted and packaged the fish for delivery to faraway lands.

Magdala was also the hometown of Mary Magdalene, the woman from whom Christ cast out seven demons. We do not know what kind of demons afflicted her. There is nothing in the Bible to indicate she was a prostitute, as is sometimes claimed. Mary Magdalene became one of Christ's most ardent followers and was one of the few who stood by him beneath the cross.

Fishermen had to be bold to deal with the storms on the lake. They also had to have some knowledge of both Greek and Latin. They learned it at an early age, for fishing was a trade handed down from father to son. By law, they had to count their fish and pay taxes on their catch. In sum, the apostle fishermen were down to earth men skilled at fishing as well as marketing their product. Their work was a necessary part of the economy, but their social standing was little better than unskilled laborers. Most of the time, they smelled like fish.

Christ's followers didn't know how his mission would end. Most of them probably believed that He was the messiah who would bring justice and would deliver Israel from the Romans. Then came Christ's triumphant entry into Jerusalem. He chose to ride on a lowly ass, not the expectation of a conqueror, but to the people it made little difference. They tore palm fronds from branches and threw down their cloaks on the road, shouting "Hosanna, Hosanna" to their messiah, the one who would deliver them from oppression. Who would not be impressed by the crowd rejoicing at his entry into Jerusalem?

Why, one might ask, did the enthusiastic crowd turn against Jesus a few days later? For one thing, they were different Jews. These Jews were people coming into the city of Jerusalem for the Passover from all parts of the country. They saw Jesus as their savior, and they fully anticipated that he would lead a rebellion against the Romans and against the injustices of their own officials. Their very cry, "Hosanna," translated means "save now," an entreaty for Christ to lead them against oppression.

When days passed and nothing happened, those who had now arrived in Jerusalem and found places to stay may have been disappointed. However, it is not at all sure that they were the same people whom the Pharisees roused early on Friday morning to gather before Pilate and cry for the release of Barabbas and the crucifixion of Christ.

Given the welcome by the enthusiastic multitude, it is no surprise that despite Christ's warnings, the apostles were not prepared for the crucifixion. For that reason, they scurried about, hiding when Jesus was arrested. One of Christ's disciples, some think it was John, escaped without his clothes when the Jewish authorities tried to seize him by holding onto his garments. The apostles were scared that they too would be taken, and only one, John, had the courage to be present when Christ died.

His women followers had more valor. The gospels record that Mary, Mary Magdalene, Salome and Mary, the wife of Clopas were there at the cross. Another woman, Veronica, by tradition wiped the face of Jesus as he made his way to Golgotha.

Death by crucifixion is a terribly agonizing way to die. In addition, Jesus suffered a cruel scourging with whips imbedded with pieces of bone or steel as well as a crown of sharp thorns pressed into his scalp. For those who saw him, a lasting image of his suffering would have been permanently etched in their minds. No one, having witnessed the gruesome execution, would be likely to recall Christ's words that he would rise again. No one, that is, except the Pharisees and Sadducees, the religious rulers of Israel who were responsible for his death. They are the ones who went to Pilate and asked for the tomb to be guarded lest the body be removed and it be proclaimed that he had risen.

# Chapter Two
## What happened on the day of resurrection

The tomb where Jesus was laid belonged to Joseph of Arimathea. It was his own personal gravesite on land he owned that in preparation had been hollowed out of stone. John mentions that the tomb was a new one which had never been used. During this time in Judea, it was typical to reuse graves for other family members if a year or more had passed. The bones of the deceased were placed in an ossuary to make room for a new burial. A large flat rolling stone was typically made that would be rolled in front of the opening to seal the tomb.

Joseph was a member of the Sanhedrin, the priestly ruling body which had condemned and brought Jesus before Pilate. He was a follower of Christ, but secretly, for fear of most of the Sanhedrin who wanted Jesus dead. After the crucifixion, he went to see Pilate and boldly asked for Christ's body. According to the Gospel of John, Jesus was already dead when the soldiers came to break the legs of the two others crucified. Instead, one of them thrust his lance into his side to be absolutely certain of his death.

Pilate had already checked with the soldiers that Jesus had died, and so he released the body. Joseph was assisted by Nicodemus, another member of the Sanhedrin who was also a secret follower of Christ. These men, probably helped by others, took the body, along with a large quantity of spices and carried it to the tomb. They wrapped Jesus' body with myrrh and aloes in burial garments and laid him down. On the third day, actually only about 36 hours later, he arose from the grave.

There are slightly different gospel interpretations on what happened next. For some, this has been a problem. For most, it is not. We will take a look at the differences, and you can see how they vary and come to your own conclusions.

It would be easy to quote all the gospels to show what each of the evangelists wrote about the day of Christ's resurrection. However, anyone can do that simply by looking up the accounts toward the end of the gospels of Matthew, Mark, Luke and John. A close reading shows the differences.

All accounts of the resurrection agree that it happened quite early in the morning, and in fact, in John the sun had not yet risen. Different people are named as witnesses. All the gospels include Mary Magdalene. For John, she was the only one there, while for two of the synoptic authors, Mark and Luke, Mary Magdalene was accompanied by Mary, the mother of James. Matthew probably includes her also, but he just says, "the other Mary" in his gospel. Mark and Luke include others. For Mark it is Salome and for Luke it is Joanna and others.

What do these women see when they arrive? Mark and Matthew report that the women see a young man, (Mark's gospel), and an angel, (Matthew's gospel.) Luke says the women see two men and John says Mary Magdalene sees two angels. It is apparent that the women don't know if the people they see are angels or only men. All the gospels show that those they see are garbed in white.

In each of the synoptic gospels, the beings in white tell the women that Jesus has been raised from the dead. They are to tell this to the disciples. John's gospel, however, is different. In his version, Mary Magdalene goes to the tomb and finding that the stone has been rolled back, she runs to tell Peter and one other unnamed disciple. They run to the tomb, enter, and see burial cloths—the head piece of which is rolled up and placed in a separate place. The apostles leave, and based on John's story, Mary Magdalene returns but does not immediately enter the tomb.

This is how the gospel of John tells the story; the only gospel to mention this scene. "But Mary was standing outside near the tomb, weeping. Then, as she wept, she stooped to look inside, and saw two angels in white sitting where the body of Jesus had been, one at the head, the other at the feet. They said, 'Woman, why are you weeping?' 'They have taken my Lord away,' she replied, 'and I don't know where they have put him.' As she said this, she turned round and saw Jesus standing there, though she did not recognize it was Jesus. Jesus said to her, 'Woman, why are you weeping? Who are you looking for?' Supposing him to be the gardener, she said, 'Sir, if you have taken him away, tell me where you have put him.' Jesus said, 'Mary!' She turned round then and said to him in Hebrew, 'Rabbuni!— which means master. Jesus said to her, 'Do not cling to me, because I have not yet ascended to the Father. But go and find my brothers, and tell them I am ascending to my Father and your Father, to my God and your God.' So Mary of Magdala told the disciples, 'I have seen the Lord,' and that he had said these things to her." (John 20:11-18)

Anyone who has read the gospels knows that John's gospel is different. All three of the other accounts of Jesus' life attempt to describe Christ's life and teachings in a concrete, matter of fact way. They show that the apostles only very gradually came to an awareness that Christ was the Son of God. In general, there is agreement among them, though one or the other includes scenes left out of the other accounts.

John breaks the mold. From the very beginning of his gospel, Jesus is recognized as God. Moreover, instead of telling parables, in John Christ speaks at length to the apostles of their relationship to Him, the Father and the Holy Spirit. This is especially true at the last supper. Chapters fourteen through seventeen are entirely Christ's instructions to his disciples.

John is an interesting person in his own right. Jesus called him and his brother, James "sons of thunder" (Mark 3:17). They are vibrant personalities. At one point, when Jesus was not well received by the Samaritans, these brothers asked Jesus, "Lord, do you want us to call down fire from heaven to burn them up?" (Luke 9:54)

Their mother, Salome, was no less bold. She came, bowing before Jesus with her two sons to make a request of him. Jesus asked her, "What is it you want?' She said to him, 'Promise that these two sons of mine may sit one at your right hand and the other at your left hand in your kingdom.'(Matt 20:21) It is evident that even at this time in his ministry, the apostles, at least James, John and their mother, are thinking that Jesus will establish his kingdom on earth and they want to be honored as his chief officials.

The gospel of John is generally accepted to be authored or handed down by the very same apostle who was with Christ throughout his travels. John may well have been the youngest of the apostles, as the gospels assert he is the younger brother of James, sons of Zebedee. His mother, Salome, is mentioned by Mark as one of the women who was at the tomb at the resurrection.

The gospel of John is unique in being the only one to tell of the wedding at Cana, the Samaritan woman at the well, the raising of

Lazarus, and the washing of the disciples' feet. John's accurate description of many of the actual places in Jerusalem, which by 70AD was destroyed by the Romans, shows he was there at the scene. By tradition and some gospel evidence, he is the only apostle who was not martyred. He is also thought to be the same John to whom Christ from the cross gave the responsibility of caring for his mother, Mary.

However, there is what appears to be a major difference in John's gospel. The last supper happens on the wrong day! In the gospels of Mark, Luke, and Matthew, Christ and his apostles prepare to celebrate the Passover supper on the first day of the Passover. In John, a supper takes place on the day before the Passover, and there is no mention that it is a Passover meal. Even more significantly, in John's gospel Christ does not bless the bread and give it to the apostles saying, "This is my body." In fact, in the Gospel of John, there is no institution of the Eucharist. Instead, Christ washes the disciples' feet as his example to them of how Christians should serve others.

Many have tried in various ways to explain the difference in John's gospel. One is that he did not intend for it to be a literal day-by-day description of events. Most biblical scholars say that John's Gospel was the last one written, perhaps decades after the other gospels.

It is evident that John, or his followers wanted to focus more on the spiritual and theological significance of Christ's mission on earth. Some scholars believe he chose the wrong day for a reason; to show that Christ's death came

on the very day and hour when traditionally the
lambs were slaughtered in preparation for the
Jewish Passover Feast. Christ thus becomes the
new sacrificial lamb, the lamb sacrificed for our
salvation.

## The road to Emmaus

Returning to the day of the resurrection,
the gospels of Mark and especially Luke tell the
story of Jesus' appearance to two other witnesses.
It is Sunday in Jerusalem, the Passover
celebrations are over, and like many other Jews
who celebrated the feast there, two men are
returning home. Luke's gospel tells us that the
small town they are returning to is named
Emmaus, and it is about seven miles distant from
Jerusalem. The men are traveling by foot, the
usual way to travel during biblical times. We can
imagine that walking at a good but unhurried
pace the trip would take two to three hours.
One of the men is named Cleopas, and the
other is left unnamed. Jesus joins them as they
travel. We know from the gospel the men are
discouraged because of Christ's execution. We also
know from Luke's account that they are in some
way associated with the women at the tomb and
with the disciples. The following excerpt from the
gospel makes this clear. Speaking to Jesus, whom
they didn't recognize, they say:
"...and some women from our group have
astounded us: they went to the tomb in the early

morning, and when they could not find the body, they came back to tell us that they had seen a vision of angels who declared he was alive. Some of our friends went to the tomb and found everything exactly as the women had reported, but of him they saw nothing." (Luke 24:22-24)

It is apparent, from this description, that the two men heading toward Emmaus, while not apostles, were disciples and friends of those who were closest to Christ.

Christ then said to them, "You foolish men! So slow to believe all that the prophets have said! Was it not necessary that the Christ should suffer before entering into his glory?"(Luke 24: 25, 26)

The men still had several miles go before they would arrive at their home. Christ accompanied them, explaining to them all the scriptures relating to himself, "starting from Moses and going through all the prophets."

It is interesting that up to this point no one else except Mary Magdalene has reported seeing Christ. It may be that Christ also made an appearance to his mother, the Blessed Virgin Mary, but such a visit is not recorded. However, these men, one whose name is Cleopas and the other who is unnamed, don't know that it is Christ that is walking with them. That changes when they reach their village. They ask Christ to stay with them, pointing out "it is nearly evening and the day is almost over."

It is only when they were eating together, when Jesus took the bread and blessing it, broke it and gave it to them that they recognized him. Then he vanished from their sight.

Why didn't they recognize him before? Surely as disciples, they had often seen and heard him speaking. True, they were dejected, and may have hardly looked up when Christ was speaking to them on the road. However, Mary Magdalene also didn't recognize Jesus, thinking at first that he was the gardener. Mary Magdalene last saw Jesus when he was beaten and bloodied on the cross. If the two travelers were also at the crucifixion, they too would hardly have recognized Jesus in his resurrected body.

Excited, these men hurry back the seven miles to Jerusalem to tell the other disciples what they have witnessed.

# An aside: Islam and the resurrection

Today, Islam is the second largest religion in the world after Christianity. Surprisingly, though Muslims believe in Christ and his virgin birth, they do not believe in his resurrection. In fact, they don't believe in his crucifixion. Muslims recognize Jesus as a great prophet, but they do not believe that he is the son of God. Many Muslims believe that instead of Christ dying, another man was changed by God to look like Christ and was crucified in his stead.

Muslims accept the Pentateuch, the first five books of the Jewish and Christian Bible. However, they do not accept the New Testament. Consequently, Christ's appearances after his resurrection are also not part of their religious belief.

The Muslim religion was not founded until 622AD, and it is doubtful that the Arabs had access at that time to non-Christian historical sources such as Tacitus and Josephus that verify Christ's crucifixion independent of the New Testament.

# Chapter three
## Astonishment in the upper room

On Sunday, the first day of the week as reckoned in biblical times, the apostles are again gathered in an upper room. The doors are locked and the men there are in agitation. They are afraid the Jewish authorities will come to take them away as they have already done to their leader. Rumors are flying. Reports of sightings of the risen Christ are in the air but such stories are hard to believe. Then comes a sharp knock on the door. Immediately the apostles are seized with fear. "Who is it?" one of them says. "It is I, Cleopas," comes the answer. They know the voice, and relieved, the door is opened.

Cleopas and his companion had traveled the seven miles back to Jerusalem. They apparently know of the upper room where most of the apostles and others are staying. "We have seen the Christ!" they announce. They tell them how they met Jesus on the road and talked with him and how they recognized him at the breaking of the bread. While those there were still speaking about this, Christ entered through locked doors and appearing in their midst said to them, "Peace be with you." Startled and terrified, they thought they were seeing a ghost. (Luke 24:36, 37)

Three different gospel writers tell of this upper room meeting with Christ. Two of their accounts are quite similar, but the third adds more information. First, let us look at the similarities, and then we will see the account that is different. In the gospels of Mark, Luke and John, Christ appears to the assembled apostles. In Luke and John, he specifically says, "Peace be with you."Also, in Luke and John, he shows them his wounds, proving for them that he is Christ in bodily form and not an apparition. The apostles rejoice that Jesus is back with them.

In John's gospel, however, we see a difference that to this day separates the Catholic Church from many Protestant religions. Christ says to them, "As the Father sent me, so am I sending you." After saying this, he breathed on them and said, "Receive the Holy Spirit. If you forgive anyone's sins, they are forgiven; if you retain anyone's sins they are retained." (John 20:21-23)

This passage, and a like verse in Matthew's gospel, provides the basis for the Catholic sacrament of penance. The other verse from Matthew is: "And so I say to you, you are Peter, and upon this rock I will build my church, and the gates of the netherworld shall not prevail against it. I will give you the keys to the kingdom of heaven. Whatever you bind on earth shall be bound in heaven; and whatever you loose on earth shall be loosed in heaven." (Matthew 16:18, 19)

Confession of sins was practiced in the early days of Christianity up to the 1500's when Martin Luther took exception to many of the teachings of the church. His main complaint relating to confession was not the sacrament itself but payment for indulgences. Indulgences were actually sold during the late Middle Ages and the money was used to build churches, to help the poor, and some went into the hands of wealthy bishops. The payments for indulgences supposedly took away the punishment for sins that had been confessed.

The need to pay money for indulgences was recognized to be morally offensive and was finally rescinded by the Catholic Church in 1571. However, indulgences remain, and those who are interested can still receive them by saying certain prayers, doing works of charity, making personal sacrifices, etc.

Returning to confession, the Catholic Church is now the only mainstream church that elevates confession or Penance, as it is called, to the status of a major sacrament. However, even within this church there have been substantial changes. The black box, where the penitent told their sins to a priest they couldn't see is often replaced by face to face confession. Moreover, most Catholics don't confess their sins nearly as often as they did years ago. Weekly, or biweekly confession on Saturday afternoon is for most a thing of the past.

Instead, many Catholics go only a few times a year, some only once or twice a year, usually at the approach of Christmas or Easter. A new method of reconciliation has almost become the norm. As Christmas or Easter approaches, a pastor from one church invites other priests from the area to come to his parish for a communal penance service. Parishioners are informed of the date and time, and arrive for the "penitential service" which includes prayers and often music.

The numerous priests station themselves at various locations, and the faithful form lines sufficiently far from their priest of choice so that while standing, or sitting, depending on the church, the penitent can softly speak their sins to the confessor. As usual, some take much longer than others, but with so many priests, the entire ceremony can take an hour or less. This is the modern confession in the Catholic Church today, at least in the United States.

# After the resurrection

Tracking Christ's movements after his resurrection is not the easiest thing to do. We have the four gospel accounts, and we also have sightings reported in the Acts of the Apostles and Paul's letter to the Corinthians. All of these authors focused on certain things that were most important to them. They are not simply recording what someone else has written. Today, we may actually have a better knowledge of the sequence of events than then, for we can put all the accounts together in what seems to be a logical order.

In the last section, we saw that Christ appeared to the apostles assembled in the upper room. We don't know for sure all who were there, but it is likely that besides the apostles there were also at least some disciples as well as women followers. Mary, the mother of Jesus is not mentioned, but she may very well have been there as well. However, we know that one important person was missing: Thomas, one of the original twelve.

One can imagine the other apostles bringing Thomas up to date, excitedly telling him that they have seen the risen Christ. Thomas remains unmoved by their revelation. Apparently, he trusts in nothing except his own eyes, for he tells them, "Unless I can see the holes that the nails made in his hands and can put my finger into the holes they made, and unless I can put my hand into his side, I refuse to believe." (John 20: 25). Many biblical scholars believe that John, the apostle, was the one who wrote or who dictated the gospel named after him. If they are correct, John was in that upper room, and no doubt, he vividly remembered the words of Thomas that day.

The fact that Thomas was still in disbelief was no doubt disconcerting to the other apostles. These men had been together for a long time; they knew each other well and they were friends. Thomas' lack of trust in them was hard for them to understand. However, the same kind of thing has probably happened to us. We have witnessed something with our own eyes that is simply amazing. We tell it to a friend, and we are surprised when they don't seem to believe us. What will it take, we may think, to open his or her eyes? A personal revelation?

With Thomas, that is exactly what happened. Eight days later the apostles were together again. This upper level room where they met is probably the same one used at the last supper and frequently thereafter. It is likely that it was owned by one of Christ's disciples. The doors are again locked when Christ appears. After saying "Peace be with you," he immediately speaks to Thomas. "Put your finger here; look, here are my hands. Give me your hand; put it into my side. Do not be believing any more but believe." (John 20:27)

"Thomas replied, 'My Lord and my God!' Jesus said to him: 'You believe because you can see me. Blessed are those who have not seen and yet believe.'"

Christ's words echo down through the centuries for all those who have not seen, but believe in him and his resurrection from the dead.

# Chapter four

## New teachings by the Sea of Galilee

One of Christ's most intriguing appearances shows a very human side of both Jesus and his apostles. At the last supper, in Matthew, and again after his resurrection Jesus tells the apostles to meet him in Galilee. Now that he has appeared to them twice in Jerusalem, they make their way back to where Christ's ministry began, the towns along the shore of Galilee and the nearby town of Nazareth. The trip is approximately 80 miles, and traveling by foot takes them at least three or four days.

Once they are in Galilee, the apostles feel much safer from their concern of being arrested by the Jewish authorities. When the Lord doesn't come immediately, Peter, a man of action, likely grew restless and decided to go back to fishing. He outfitted his boat and told the others, "I am going fishing." (John 21:3). Six of the apostles decided to go along,: James and John, Thomas, Nathanael, and two others unnamed. They fished through the night, and as John's gospel says, ". . .they caught nothing."

As the morning light was breaking, the apostles see a man in the distance on the shore. They don't know at first who it is, but his voice carries to them. "Haven't you caught anything, friends?" (John 21:5) They told him they had not and he says to them, "Throw the net out to the starboard and you'll find something."

John's gospel is very descriptive in recording what happened next. The apostles throw out the net and so many fish are caught they cannot haul them into the boat. One of the apostles, John, recognizes that it is Jesus on the shore. Peter, in a hurry to see Christ, jumps into the water and swims to Jesus while the other disciples come in on the boat dragging the net full of fish.

Once on shore, they find Jesus cooking breakfast on a charcoal fire. He has some fish grilling along with some bread and he says to them, "Bring some of the fish you just caught." Simon goes to help them get the fish ashore, and all are amazed at the catch—one hundred and fifty-three large fish. The apostles recognize Jesus, but stand around, seemingly too awed to address him. Jesus says, "Come and have breakfast."

At this point Jesus serves his disciples, handing them portions of bread and fish. After they have eaten, Christ confronts Peter. Three times, he asks him, "Do you love me." Twice Peter answers him, ""Yes, Lord, you know that I love you." When Christ asks him a third time, Peter is disturbed and answers, "Lord, you know everything; you know that I love you." On each of the three times that Peter proclaims his love, Jesus gives him an order. The first time it was, "Feed my lambs," the second, "Tend my sheep," and the third, "Feed my sheep." (John 21: 15-17)

Much has been made of this dialogue between Christ and Peter. Peter had denied Jesus three times in the courtyard of the high priest's house. Now Peter is asked three times to repudiate his denial with affirmations of love. However, there is more to it than that. With every affirmation, Christ gives Peter a directive. A directive that is quite specific, as it is repeated in slightly different versions three times.

The lambs and the sheep that Christ mentions are the faithful, or those who are called to be faithful. The lambs are the young sheep, the youthful and immature followers of Christ. They have much to learn, and they need to be nurtured as they grow in faith. The sheep are more mature, also part of the flock of Jesus. They too, must be fed and shepherded.

Why did Christ choose lambs and sheep when talking about his followers? Lambs are baby sheep, and these animals were the common animals of the people. Households of any means in smaller towns and villages would keep one or two sheep and also a goat. The goat provided milk and the sheep wool, from which women made garments. Both could, on occasion, also be used for their meat.

But, as people of that time would know, goats and sheep are very different animals. Goats have sizeable horns, which, unlike rams, grow straight from their heads. Consequently, they are much more dangerous when they butt. Their hair is much shorter and does not ordinarily need to be shorn. They are curious animals and like to explore and often find a way to get over or through fences. They are much more independent than sheep. In fact, unlike domesticated sheep, they can live a long time without a shepherd's help.

In contrast, sheep are sociable animals that are most content when among large groups of other sheep as they graze in meadows. They are basically defenseless, and therefore prey to wolves, jackals and hyenas. Their wool grows so long and heavy that they are unable to right themselves if they fall down. If they wander off from the herd, they have no sense of direction to find their way back.

In chapter twenty-five of Matthew's gospel Jesus uses an example of how shepherds separate the sheep from the goats. When Christ compares people to these animals, it is the goats that do not fare well, because they have not cared for those in need. In this parable, the sheep receive eternal reward because they are actively concerned with the needs of others. (See Matthew, 25:32-46)

Christ reached out to all peoples. In John, (10:16) He said, "And there are other sheep I have that are not of this fold, and I must lead these too."

Christ also said, "I am the good shepherd." (John 9: 11) He affirmed that the good shepherd is willing, if necessary, to lay down his life for his sheep. That is what Christ did on Calvary. His message to Peter that morning on the shore is a clear statement on how he wanted his Church to be governed. He wants the faithful to be shepherded by good shepherds.

# Chapter five
## An unusual account, and a new mandate

Some could say, based on much of the gospels, that Christ's message was limited to the Jews. There is a great deal of evidence to support their claims. One dramatic account shows this clearly. It is the story of Christ and the Syro-Phoenician woman, (Canaanite) recorded in the gospels of both Mark and Matthew. For many of us, this is not the Christ we know, the one we assume is loving and caring for all people. Probably the best way to look at this is to show exactly what is recorded in the Gospel of Matthew:

"Jesus left that place and withdrew to the region of Tyre and Sidon. And suddenly out came a Canaanite woman from that district and started shouting, 'Lord, Son of David, take pity on me. My daughter is tormented by a devil.' But he said not a word in answer to her. And his disciples went and pleaded with him, saying, 'Give her what she wants, because she keeps shouting after us.' He said in reply, 'I was sent only to the lost sheep of the House of Israel.' But the woman had come up and was bowing low before him. 'Lord,' she said, 'help me.' He replied, 'It is not fair to take the children's food and throw it to little dogs.' She retorted, 'Ah yes, Lord; but even the little dogs eat the scraps that fall from their masters' table.'

Then Jesus answered her, 'Woman, you have great faith. Let your desire be granted.' And from that moment her daughter was well again." Matt 15: 22-28.


What are we to make of this story? This is one of many accounts where Jesus limits his teaching and miracles to Israel. Personally, I like the pluck and the quick thinking of this woman. She talks back to Christ to get what she wants. She cares only for her daughter, and even accepting the appellation of "little dog," she retorts that dogs eat the scraps from their master's table. But why did Jesus initially refuse to help her?

Of course, there are all kinds of analyses out there. One says that Jesus in his human nature made a mistake. He didn't do the right thing at the time. However, that Christ could actually make such a human mistake is unbelievable to many Christians.

Most commentaries state that Jesus and his apostles had left the Holy Land to go to a place where they were not known to get some much needed rest. However, the Canaanite woman learned of his coming and began yelling from outside the house for him to help her. Is it any wonder Jesus at first ignored her?

Another theory is that Jesus was testing the woman. By appearing indifferent to her need, he was making the point for her and for those who read her story of the necessity of being persistent in prayers and petitions to God.

Regardless, the message is clear. Jesus during most of his ministry wanted to limit his teaching to the Jews. In fact, when he sent his apostles out to preach this is what he told them:

'Do not make your way to gentile territory, and do not enter any Samaritan town; go instead to the lost sheep of the House of Israel.'"(Matt 10:5)

## The last resurrection appearances

We now come to the last resurrection appearances of Christ. The reports come from different places in scripture. Most are short, non-descriptive entries. In Corinthians, 15: 6, 7, Paul mentions that the risen Christ appeared to 500 at once, and in the next line that he appeared to James. The evangelist Luke, in his Acts of the Apostles, chapter one, says, "He presented himself alive to them by many proofs after he had suffered, appearing to them during forty days and speaking about the kingdom of God."

In at least one of his appearances, Christ tells the apostles to wait in Jerusalem where they "will be baptized with the Holy Spirit." (Acts 1:5 and Luke 23:49)

After the resurrection, in one of his last appearances to the apostles, Christ gives them a new mission. Suddenly, it seems, Christ no longer wants to limit his message to the Jews. Instead, his disciples are instructed to go out into the whole world. This is what Jesus says:
"Go, therefore, and make disciples of all nations, baptizing them in the name of the Father, and of the Son, and of the holy Spirit, teaching them to observe all that I have commanded you." (Matt 28:19,20)

In Mark 16, he says, "Go into the whole world and proclaim the gospel to every creature." In Luke, Christ says, "Thus it is written that the Messiah would suffer and rise from the dead on the third day and that repentance, for the forgiveness of sins, would be preached in his name to all the nations, beginning from Jerusalem." (Luke 23:46,47)

Jesus reluctance, before his resurrection, to bring his message to any other people than Jews is not easy to explain. It is possible that in his resurrected body, free from the limitations of a human body, he understood more fully that the message of God should go out to the whole world. Alternatively, he may have wanted the chosen people, the Jews, to receive the message first. Regardless, it is clear that even after his death, the leaders of the new church he founded at first saw the mission as being to the Jews. That soon changed, and the first council, the Council of Jerusalem in the year 50, formally decided that people other than Jews could become full members of the church without the need for them to be circumcised, or to follow other specific laws made for the Jews.

# Chapter six

## The Ascension, and the coming of the Spirit

The ascension of Christ into heaven was a major event for those who had followed Christ. It marks the end of his earthly mission and the beginning of his church, founded to carry on his message to the world. Christ at the last supper told the apostles he would be leaving them. This announcement created much grief. Jesus was their friend and leader, and the apostles did not want to see him go. They wanted to go with him. Jesus told them it was better that he leave: "But I tell you the truth, it is better for you that I go. For if I do not go, the Advocate will not come to you. But if I go, I will send him to you." (John 16:7)

In an earlier discussion with the apostles, Christ told them: "In my Father's house there are many dwelling places. If there were not, would I have told you that I am going to prepare a place for you? And if I go and prepare a place for you, I will come back again and take you to myself, so that where I am going you may also be." (John 14:2-3)

The actual ascension scene is described in Mark, Luke, and in the Acts of the Apostles. The Acts of the Apostles account is the most descriptive: Christ said to them, ". . .but you will receive the power of the Holy Spirit which will come on you, and then you will be my witnesses not only in Jerusalem but throughout Judaea and Samaria, and indeed to earth's remotest end."

"As he said this he was lifted up while they looked on, and a cloud took him from their sight. They were still staring into the sky as he went when suddenly two men in white were standing beside them and they said, 'Why are you Galileans standing here looking into the sky? This Jesus who has been taken up from you into heaven will come back in the same way as you have seen him go to heaven.' (Acts 1:8-11)

Afterwards, the apostles left the small mountain from where he had risen, Mount Olivet. It is located on the outskirts of the old city overlooking Jerusalem. From there the apostles walked down the short distance to return to Jerusalem

Though the apostles and many disciples, both men and women, followed Christ's directions and waited in Jerusalem for the Holy Spirit, few knew what to expect. In addition, there is uncertainty about the details of the Holy Spirit's coming. Acts 2 says: ". . .they had all met together, when suddenly there came from heaven a sound as of a violent wind which filled the entire house in which they were sitting;" Note that the number of people gathered together is not mentioned. Some think it was one hundred and twenty people, the number of men mentioned in Acts 1 who voted on who would succeed Judas as one of the twelve apostles. However, that vote was taken on another day, before the Holy Spirit came.

On Pentecost day, Acts, 2:2-13 tells what happened: ". . .and there appeared to them tongues as of fire; these separated and came to rest on the head of each of them. They were all filled with the Holy Spirit and began to speak different languages as the Spirit gave them power to express themselves."

Then, the second chapter of Acts enumerates all the peoples and all the languages that the Jews hear the apostles speaking: "Then how does each of us hear them in his own native language? We are Parthians, Medes and Elamites, inhabitants of Mesopotamia, Judea and Cappadocia, Pontus and Asia, of Libya near Cyrene, as well as travelers from Rome, both Jews and converts to Judaism, Cretans and Arabs, yet we hear them speaking in our own tongues of the mighty acts of God."

All these Jews from different countries are "astounded and bewildered" for they know the apostles are Galileans, who among the Jewish people are not known for being well educated. They are filled with wonder, except for a few who scoff and say, "They have had too much wine."

## The Holy Spirit came: what changed?

Most, if not all Christian religions today have a belief in the Holy Spirit. One branch, the Pentecostals, even take their name from the day the Spirit came down, on Pentecost. Staunch belief in the Holy Spirit is continuous throughout history into our own time. The Catholic Church has a definitive sacrament, Confirmation, with laying on of hands and anointing with blessed oil to impart the Holy Spirit. We might wonder, how did its reception change things in the early church? How does it change things today? What are the signs of the Holy Spirit, and, on a more personal level, how is one to know if the Holy Spirit is active or not in our lives?

# Chapter seven
## The effect of the Holy Spirit on the apostles

Although we don't know exactly how many apostles and others initially received the Holy Spirit, the effect was almost immediate. The apostles, who apparently had spent much time in the upper room, were now emboldened and left the house to preach. Led by Peter, the eleven apostles stood up before a crowd of Jews to speak. The first thing Peter told them was, "These people are not drunk, as you suppose, for it is only nine o'clock in the morning." (Acts 2:15)

Then Peter quotes from the prophet Joel in which he says, "I will pour out a portion of my **spirit** on all flesh." Again, Peter emphasizes, "God's **spirit** will be poured out on all, including "servants and handmaids." (Acts 2:17, 18)

After telling the crowd that the prophesy of the coming of the Holy Spirit has been fulfilled in their own time, Peter proceeds to speak to them of Jesus crucified and raised from the dead. He points out that Christ is the promised Messiah, and that he is greater than their great King David, whose remains are buried in a tomb. Finally, he tells them, "Repent and be baptized, every one of you, in the name of Jesus Christ for the forgiveness of your sins; and you [also] will receive the gift of the Holy **Spirit**." (Acts 2:38)

Peter's sermon to the Jews is much longer than is recorded here, and more of it is included in Acts, chapter two. The result of the eloquence of his preaching is that "about three thousand persons" accepted his message and were baptized that day.

In the days that followed, Peter and the apostles continued to preach, and they were also able to effect miraculous cures. However, before many days passed they were arrested by temple guards and placed in prison. The following day they were warned not to preach in the name of Christ anymore. Peter and John told the members of the Sanhedrin, "Whether it is right in the sight of God for us to obey you rather than God, you be the judges. It is impossible for us not to speak about what we have seen and heard." (Acts 4:19, 20)

It is not hard to imagine that with this type of attitude it would not be long before the apostles would have further trouble with the authorities. Israel was a religious state and consequently all law, except that imposed by the conquering Romans, was religious law. The ruling body of Jerusalem was the Sanhedrin, composed of seventy men and an elected high priest. They had their own soldiers, or police, as well as their own public jail.

The apostles and many other Christianized Jews continued to meet in one of the large porticos of the temple. From there they would go to different houses to break bread. More and more of the Jews were being won over to the new faith. The high priest and his influential friends became jealous of their success and again had the apostles arrested and put in jail. According to Acts, an angel released them that same night and the next day found the apostles again teaching in the temple.

In consternation, the religious authorities brought them back and made them stand before the Sanhedrin where the high priest questioned them. He told them, "We gave you strict orders [did we not] to stop teaching in that name. Yet you have filled Jerusalem with your teaching and want to bring this man's blood upon us." (Acts 5: 28)

The apostles, the same men who had previously hidden behind locked doors in the upper room, were now fearless in front of this body of men who had the power to take their lives. Their answer was, "We must obey God rather than men. The God of our ancestors raised Jesus, though you had him killed by hanging him on a tree. God exalted him at his right hand as leader and savior to grant Israel repentance and forgiveness of sins. We are witnesses of these things, as is the Holy Spirit that God has given to those who obey him." (Acts 5:29-32)

You might imagine the affect these unlettered fishermen had as they lectured those most esteemed men of the priestly class of all Israel. Acts states "They became infuriated and wanted to put them to death."

One man saved them. A Pharisee named Gamaliel, who was also a member of the Sanhedrin, stood up to speak. Luke says he was "respected by all the people." Before he spoke, he had the apostles taken outside. Without going over his full argument, which is given in chapter five of Acts, Gamaliel made this point: He told the men of the Sanhedrin that in the past, others had attracted converts to their beliefs, but their religious movements did not in the end amount to anything. Then he told them that if this activity is of men it will destroy itself. However, if it is of God, you will not be able to destroy it.

Gamaliel was successful in turning the Sanhedrin from their murderous intent. However, still simmering with anger, they had the apostles flogged, and then released them, reiterating that they were never again to speak in the name of Jesus.

The whipping the apostles endured was not with the flagellum, the multi tailed whip imbedded with steel or bone that Christ suffered.

The whip used by the Jews did not tear away the flesh. However, it left lasting welts that would remain on their backs for the rest of their lives. Acts says that the apostles rejoiced afterwards that they had been found worthy to suffer for Christ. Such was their fervor after the coming of the Holy Spirit.

Another of the disciples did not fare so well. Stephen was working "great signs and wonders among the people." While he was preaching, some Jews who were visiting in Jerusalem debated with him. It seems he was winning the debates, for a number of those present brought false charges against him that he was blaspheming both Moses and God.

Stephen was brought before the Sanhedrin, and in answer to their questioning, he began a quite longwinded discourse describing God's actions from Abraham, to Joseph, Moses, David and Solomon. He ended with words that could only infuriate members of the Sanhedrin. He said, "You stubborn people, with uncircumcised hearts and ears. You are always resisting the Holy Spirit, just as your ancestors used to do. Can you name a single prophet your ancestors never persecuted? They killed those who foretold the coming of the Upright One, and now you have become his betrayers, his murderers. In spite of being given the Law through angels, you have not kept it." (Acts 7: 41-53)

The Sanhedrin had heard enough. For them, things had come to a head and they were ready to sentence him. Then, Stephen continued even more dramatically. "Look! I can see heaven thrown open and the Son of man standing at the right hand of God."

These words enraged the Sanhedrin, who rushed at him, and leading him out of the city, they stoned him to death. Not content with killing Stephen, that very day the Sanhedrin and their followers began a bitter persecution against Christians. As Acts 8: 1 says, ". . .everyone except the apostles scattered to the country districts of Judaea and Samaria." Saul, known later as Paul after his miraculous conversion, "went from house to house arresting both men and women and sending them to prison." (Acts 8: 3).

The fact that the Jews killed Stephen and that later King Herod beheaded the apostle James goes against what the Jews told Pilate. "We do not have the right to execute anyone." (John 18:31) The Jews certainly put people to death. Remember the incident of the woman caught in adultery. The Jews were ready to stone her to death when Christ intervened and said, "Let the one among you who is without sin be the first to throw a stone at her." (John 8:7) The Jews could execute people, but their law did not allow them to crucify anyone. Christ's enemies wanted Jesus to suffer the most agonizing death.

One major effect of the persecution in Jerusalem was that the new faith began to spread to other areas. As it was no longer safe for Christians to stay in Jerusalem, those who wished to tell others of their faith moved on to other towns.

Saul, whose Latinized name is Paul, was one of the most zealous persecutors of Christians.

As Acts records, "He was trying to destroy the church; entering house after house and dragging out men and women, he handed them over for imprisonment." (Acts 8:3)

Saul recognized that Christians were leaving the city to preach elsewhere. He prepared to go Damascus, which had a large Jewish community, a city to where many escaping Christians were fleeing. Before setting out, Saul obtained letters from the high priest addressed to the synagogues in Damascus. He had every intention of bringing back Christians to Jerusalem in chains.

It was while making this journey that he was dramatically converted. Acts, chapter nine, describes what happened. Many Christians already know the story. "While he was traveling to Damascus and approaching the city, suddenly a light from heaven shone round him. He fell to the ground, and then he heard a voice saying, 'Saul, Saul, why are you persecuting me?' 'Who are you, Lord?' he asked, and the answer came, 'I am Jesus, whom you are persecuting. Get up and go into the city, and you will be told what you are to do.' The men travelling with Saul stood there speechless, for though they heard the voice they could see no one. Saul got up from the ground, but when he opened his eyes he could see nothing at all, and they had to lead him into Damascus by the hand." (Acts 9: 3-9)

Saul's conversion is a good example of how, through the power of God, a person can completely change. Zealous to the point of extremism in tracking down Christians, afterward he worked tirelessly to spread the gospel. Well educated, speaking several languages, he was also a craftsman, skilled in making tents. Though not one of the original twelve apostles, he became known as the "apostle to the gentiles." His letters to the newly founded Christian churches located in major cities of the time are included in the Bible. They were penned before any of the four major gospels were written.

As for the apostles, in their fervor to spread the gospel, they traveled over much of the then known world. They preached the gospel wherever they went and most were martyred for their faith. The following map gives a good idea of their travels.

# Map - Traditional Locations Where the Apostles Preached and Died

Key: + - the traditional place(s) of death of the Apostles and John the Baptist
Most of the locations where the Apostles preached and died come from various ancient traditions.
Paul's travels are recorded in the Acts of the Apostles

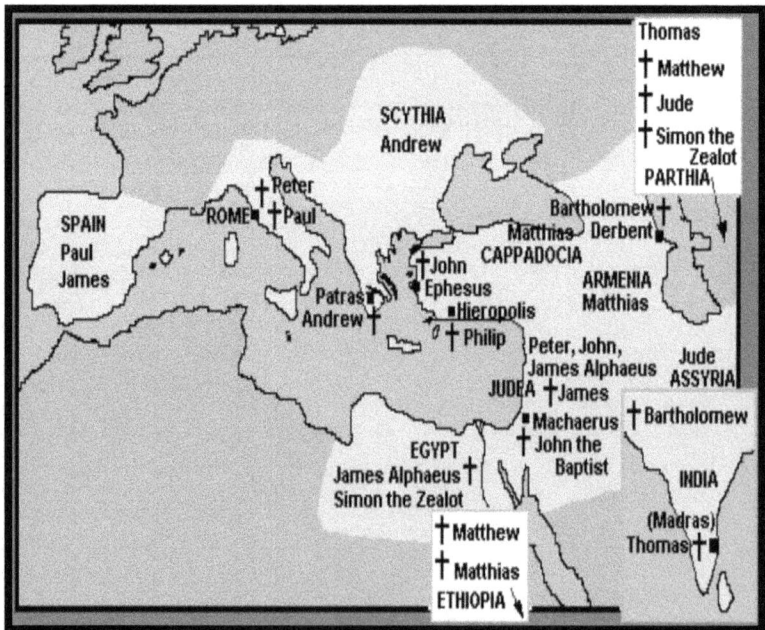

# Chapter eight

## The effect of the Holy Spirit today

We have seen the effect of receiving the Holy Spirit on the apostles. Does the Holy Spirit still come today and if so how? Is the grace received by all Christians, and those of other religions as well, or do only a privileged few receive the Holy Spirit?

Among the Christian churches today, there is great variety in how the Holy Spirit is received. Some, such as Roman Catholic, Eastern Orthodox, Oriental Orthodox, and many Anglican churches celebrate Confirmation as a sacrament and confer Confirmation at a certain time and with a specific ritual.

In America and in most Western countries, confirmation takes place when a child has at least reached the age of reason, which, depending on interpretation, can be as young as seven years old. It is administered by the laying on of hands and anointing with blessed oil by the celebrant in imparting the Holy Spirit. The age of reception varies from seven as a minimum up to as old as late teens, and unconfirmed adults can be confirmed at any age.

Other Christian churches, such as Lutherans, Methodists and Presbyterians, do not officially make confirmation a sacrament. However, for them it is a rite whereby those being confirmed are engaged in a period of instruction before they make a public profession of faith.

Many people today, while professing a belief in God, are not members of a church, or are members of a church that has no rite of confirmation. Can these people receive the Holy Spirit? It would be wrong and unbiblical to say no. Certainly, the Holy Spirit has been active in the world long before Christ founded the church. The Bible itself is an inspired work whose authors were guided by the Holy Spirit.

Yet, practically speaking, how could an unchurched person hope to receive the gifts of the Spirit? The same way as a Christian. As Christ said, "And I tell you, ask and you will receive; seek and you will find; knock and the door will be opened to you.. . . If you then, evil as you are, know how to give your children what is good, how much more will the heavenly Father give the Holy Spirit to those who ask him!" (Luke 11:9,13)

## Benefits of receiving the Holy Spirit

The advantages of receiving the Holy Spirit do not seem to be well known. Those of us who were confirmed while young may not have realized the significance of the event. As adults, we are probably better able to grasp the importance.

One person, who very early on sought the power of the Holy Spirit, was Simon, a magician. His story is quite unusual. The man practiced magic in Samaria, in the same area where Christ had the dialogue with the woman at the well. Simon made a name for himself there because he was quite an accomplished magician. In fact, as recorded in Acts, some said of him, "This man is the power of God. . ."

It happened at that time, that the apostle Philip was in the area preaching and baptizing. According to Acts, Simon himself believed in Christ and was baptized. Simon observed that not only was Philip baptizing, but mighty deeds were occurring. As Acts records, Simon was "astounded" at what he saw.

Philip's preaching in Samaria was so successful that the apostles in Jerusalem heard of it and Peter and John came to the town and prayed that those who were newly baptized might receive the Holy Spirit. Then they laid hands on

them and they received the Holy Spirit. On seeing
this, Simon offered them money if they would give
him the power. The following is what Peter said to
him:

"May your money perish with you, because
you thought that you could buy the gift of God
with money. You have no share or lot in this
matter, for your heart is not upright before God.
Repent of this wickedness of yours and pray to the
Lord that, if possible, your intention will be
forgiven. For I see that you are filled with bitter
gall and are in the bonds of iniquity." (Acts 8:20-
23)

We do not know what happened to Simon
after this rebuke by Peter. He is not mentioned
again in the New Testament. He may have
repented and gone on to live a Christian life, or he
may only have become a Christian for self-serving
reasons. Regardless, he saw the value of the gifts
of the Spirit. What did he witness that made him
lust for the power?

The gifts of the Spirit are many, and
certainly not all are given to each person. If we
know what they are, it is not hard to guess which
of them particularly interested Simon. In reality,
there are two main lists for these gifts. The
largest number of them, nine, Paul sets out in his
first letter to the Corinthians. There he says, "To
each individual the manifestation of the Spirit is
given for some benefit. To one is given through the
Spirit the expression of wisdom; to another the
expression of knowledge according to the same
Spirit; to another faith by the same Spirit; to
another gifts of healing by the one Spirit; to

another the working of <u>miracles</u>; to another <u>prophecy</u>; to another <u>discernment</u> <u>of spirits</u>; to another varieties of <u>tongues</u>; to another <u>interpretation of tongues</u>. (1 Cor 12:8-10)

Paul's list of gifts is accepted by many Protestant denominations, but other churches, including the Roman Catholic Church, use another source. They, go back approximately 700 years before Christ to cite the prophet Isaiah's listing of gifts. Looking forward to the coming Messiah, Isaiah says, "On him will rest the spirit of Yahweh, the spirit of <u>Wisdom</u> and <u>insight</u>, the spirit of <u>counsel</u> and <u>power</u>, the spirit of <u>knowledge</u> and <u>fear of Yahweh</u>." (Isaiah, 11:2, 3) The inclusion of <u>piety</u> is ordinarily added to make the total seven.

In looking at these gifts, we can see how opposed they are to vices, many of which Paul names: "Now the works of the flesh are obvious: immorality, impurity, licentiousness, idolatry, sorcery, hatreds, rivalry, jealousy, outbursts of fury, acts of selfishness, dissensions, factions, occasions of envy, drinking bouts, orgies, and the like." (Gal 5:19-21)

Today, as in every age, we see much of this kind of behavior. It is abundantly present on TV, in the movies and in the newspapers. It is present among those we know and even in our own lives. The battle between the life of the Spirit and that of the flesh is constant. It is the reason Christ came on earth to live, to preach the good news and to die for our sins.

Paul continues, in the same chapter to show the fruits, or the graces that flow from reception of the gifts of the Spirit. "In contrast, the fruit of the Spirit is

**love,
joy,
peace,
patience,
kindness,
generosity,
faithfulness,
gentleness,
self-control."**

(Print size increased for emphasis..(Gal 5:22, 23)

We probably know people who exemplify these gifts of the Holy Spirit. They are kind, friendly, and always seem to be in self-control even when things don't go as planned. They are patient, they seem wise in ordinary ways, and even in the face of adversity, they can usually see a silver lining. Why? Because they have great trust in God. They know that God loves them and cares for them. Even when other things go wrong, they know God's love for them is constant. These people are good examples of the Spirit working in their lives.

The advantages of a Spirit filled life are many. It seems that most human beings have a strong need for self-esteem. This need has been identified by many well known psychologists as William James, Abraham Maslow and Carl

Rogers. Most people are hurt and discouraged by insults whether directed at our person, our house, our clothes, our haircut, or even our car. The need for self-esteem is an important element in our striving to be successful in work, in sports and in our families. However, like anything, it can be overdone. Life can be unsatisfying if the striving for success and material things takes too much of our time and energy. Especially if it takes us away from enjoying family and friends.

Maslow is specific that after our basic needs for food, shelter and security are met, we need love and belonging. The graces that flow from the Holy Spirit help to fulfill that need, even if at times friends, family or spousal relationships leave something to be desired.

Those who were confirmed as children, may, years later, experience more of the fruits or graces of the Spirit through leading an upright life. The yearly cycle of the church: Christmas, then Easter followed by Pentecost is inspiring to many. Christ told his disciples on the eve of his crucifixion,
". . .it is for your own good that I am going, because unless I go, the Paraclete [Holy Spirit] will not come to you." (John, 16:7)

Jesus saw the indwelling of the Spirit in the lives of his followers as more consequential than his being with them in person. In the Gospel of Luke, chapter eleven, Christ tells his disciples to pray for the coming of the Holy Spirit. For Christ, those who follow him are not fully Christian until and unless the Holy Spirit is active in our lives. But is He? Do our lives exhibit the fruits of the Holy Spirit? That is, love, joy, peace, patience, kindness, generosity, faithfulness, gentleness, self-control. For most of us, the answer may be "sometimes."

We all have situations and people who at times make our lives difficult. The boss who asks too much, the relative who gets on our nerves. A spouse, teenager, or parent who doesn't listen, or is much too critical. A rambunctious or disobedient child who needs correction and guidance. As human beings, we have these situations and more to deal with.

It's hard to be kind when someone is pushing our buttons, seemingly trying to upset us. It's hard to be patient and to talk things out instead of reacting in anger. It's hard to be generous if we feel it's their own fault that people are in poor circumstances.

For these reasons and others, it may be difficult to ask the Holy Spirit to come more fully into our lives. It is easy to become satisfied with ourselves. To become satisfied with our impatience, with our temper, with our prejudices. With our accustomed way of interacting with others.

Yet, if we want to follow in the way of Christ, we need to take on the virtues he wants for us. We need to ask for his help. We need to ask Him to help us to be more like Him. We need to ask Him to help us acquire the virtues of the Holy Spirit, which he wants each of us to be blessed with. He wants us to ask for these virtues, but to do so is not always easy. It takes faith, and trust in God to allow Him to become more active in our lives.

We **dare** to ask for the gifts of the Holy Spirit, knowing we could be changed—for the better. A simple prayer, a one-liner, is all that is needed. God hears. But once is not enough. We are not like angels, so wise, that once a decision is made, we live forever as angels or devils. (See note 1) Or, in our case, as holy or unholy people. During the course of our lives, we will have many, many failings, and also much good that we will do. That's why we need to keep asking God into our lives, because we forget, become distracted, and lose our way. It is our human nature. Thankfully, God is good and loving, and knows how difficult it is for us to stay on course.

For the above reason, prayers of invocation to the Spirit are included near the end of this book.

What happens when one who is confirmed commits serious sin? Does the Spirit remain? The Spirit does remain but is "quenched" (1 Thess 5: 19) so that the Third Person is no longer as active in our lives. Until one repents, the Spirit does not completely depart, but remains only in the background and the gifts of the Spirit are hidden.

Sincere repentance is necessary, as is striving to avoid sin and temptation in the future. However, God is merciful, and knows that human beings are creatures of habit, and rooting out habitual sin is seldom easy. Even St. Paul, in his letter to the Romans admitted the difficulty. He said, "For I do not do the good I want, but the evil

I do not want." Paul continued to elaborate on this subject in his letter to the Romans, chapter seven. Christ underscored how we are to be forgiving of others in answer to Peter's question: "Lord, how often must I forgive my brother if he wrongs me? As often as seven times?" Jesus answered, 'Not seven, I tell you, but seventy-seven times.' (Matt 18: 21, 22)

# Appendix I

## Christianity and atheistic science

Most of the different Christian religions, including Catholicism, have concluded that evolutionary theory is not diametrically opposed to faith. It can be accepted as part of God's plan in directing life on earth. Most, if not all Christians also believe that God breathed his Spirit into man and woman giving them a soul and a sharing in the likeness of God himself.

Those who are atheists have a different view. Not believing in God, they do not accept that God created the universe. Instead, they see creation in a different way, which may be termed atheistic science. This view is popular among some scientists and others who don't believe in God. Here is a comparison of these two points of view:

# Christianity vs. atheistic science

| Christianity | Atheistic science |
| --- | --- |

## Creation

| | |
| --- | --- |
| The universe was started by a good God. | The universe came about through random forces of nature. |

## Evolution

| | |
| --- | --- |
| Either directly or over eons, God created life and all the variety of plants and animals | Life started on its own and evolved to form all the plants and animals |

## Man and woman

| | |
| --- | --- |
| God made man and woman above the apes, giving them intelligence and a soul. | Men and women evolved from the apes and gradually came to be more intelligent than other animals. |

## God

| | |
| --- | --- |
| God is real and we share in His life and love. | God is the product of an overactive imagination. |

| Christianity | Atheistic science |
|---|---|

## Prayer

Christian belief: People can pray at any time or place to a caring God.

No belief in God, but in time of need can petition friends and relatives for help.

## Morality

God wants us to love Him and to love our fellow men and women and not to sin against them.

As life is only a chance happening, there is no prescribed morality. Believe and do as you wish.

## Heaven

Heaven and immortal life await those who generally do good on earth.

There is no afterlife. We are animals and when we die our lives are over.

## Hell

Hell is the place or state of those who through their own fault live a life of evil.

There is no hell. Any punishment for wrong doing is only on earth.

# Appendix II

## Materialism and Religion

Are science and religion coming closer together?

Before the developments of science, religious views were predominant in the minds of most people. This was true thousands of years before Christ and for over a millennium after Christ. Religious views of how God created the earth and everything on it—plants, animals and man and woman, prevailed. Even in ancient Egyptian, Greek and Roman times, the actions of gods were commonly believed to control the weather, the success of the crops and even the lives of people. The Romans believed that making sacrifices to the gods was important. So much so, that Christians who would not publicly do so were persecuted and sometimes killed.

In the Middle Ages most people believed that God and the angels lived directly above the earth in heaven, and the devils lived far underground in an inferno made for them. Things began to change when Copernicus determined that the earth moved around the sun rather than vice versa. His book on the subject did little to change the perception of ordinary people because in the sixteenth century most people could not read.

Ninety years later, science and religion clashed when Galileo, in 1633 was imprisoned for declaring that the earth circled around the sun. For us today, his house imprisonment for nine years for this seems strange because science shows that the earth does indeed circle the sun. At the time, however, it was judged to go against the Bible and the teachings of the Church. As it turned out, Galileo was right and the Church was totally wrong. Finally, in 1992, Pope John Paul II exonerated Galileo, admitting the Church had made a mistake.

In the centuries after Galileo, the Church lost influence, and new scientific discoveries of major importance were made. Isaac Newton, in particular, had a profound and continuing influence on the way we think. His discovery of the force of gravity and its application to planets rotating around the sun formed the basis for our understanding of the universe. His mathematics are still important to this day for charting spaceflights to the moon and beyond. His grounding of the new science, known as classical mechanics, forms the basis for modern day thinking as well as materialism.

How this happened is interesting. Before the age of science, things of major import that happened on the earth were attributed to gods. When Christianity became the major religion of the world, things that happened were attributed to God, angels or demons. For example, a bolt of lighting striking someone dead was assumed to be caused by the devil or the anger of God.

With the discoveries of science from the sixteenth century on, people began to realize that the forces of nature are not necessarily caused by supernatural forces. More and more of these events, including tornadoes and tsunamis, came to be understood as the result of the natural forces of nature, and not necessarily devastation sent by an angry god. This concept of natural forces causing events led some to conclude that God plays no part in the creation of the earth and universe.

What changed? In the scientific world very much has changed. Newer research shows that the early scientific view of a steady state universe was completely wrong. Instead, by the late twentieth century, science had determined that the whole universe and everything in it started from nothing. Popularly known as "Big Bang Theory," it squares with observations that all the stars are moving farther apart in the same direction from a central starting point.

Big Bang Theory requires the action of a Creator, some entity powerful enough to start the process of creation in motion.

Today, the majority of astronomers and scientists believe the evidence shows that the creation of the universe started from a single point of tremendous energy about 13.8 million years ago. The theory leads many if not most people to believe that a Creator was necessarily involved in the making of the universe, the sun, the planets and Earth.

For the Earth to be precisely where it is, that is, not too close to the sun and its extreme heat, and also not too far away, with enough oxygen and even ozone to protect us from radiation seems provident, to say the least. That it is warm enough to sustain humans and plant life without being so cold that everything freezes (except in winter) is exceptional. No other known planet has such life affirming conditions.

On a much larger scale, scientists have learned that the known universe could only have happened if important constants, such as the force of gravity, the atomic weak force, the strong force and the electromagnetic force all had extremely precise values.

This "fine tuning of the universe," as it is called, means that without these precise constants, the entire observable universe and all life could not have developed. These observations have led many scientists to believe in God.

Other scientists, who choose to remain ambivalent to the existence of a Creator, make an assumption that the universe of stars and galaxies that we observe is only one of an almost infinite number of universes. They call this the "multiverse." Though there is no proof for the existence of these other universes, if an infinite number is postulated, the chance for the precise values of the constants needed for life to develop may become more feasible.

Today, with or without scientific evidence, most people believe in God. However, those who are not particularly religious continue to debate His activity in the world. Darwinian Theory has influenced many to believe that human beings are not a separate creation of God, but only higher-level apes.

Of course, it is true that there are some similarities between man, apes and monkeys, even though it is well known that humans have a much higher intelligence and in contrast to apes always walk on two feet. Other differences may not be as well known. Humans have scant hair compared to apes, but unlike them, what they do have needs to be cut. Head hair and beards eventually need to be trimmed, or they will grow so long to become a nuisance. Human females, have practically no facial hair. Only eyebrows and eyelashes stand out. Scientists to this day can only guess why this is so.

Unlike animals, people are able to make fundamental choices. Choices that can change their lives forever. To the extent that we can, we choose our personal lifestyle and that lifestyle becomes reality for us. For example, people choose whom to marry and often, when to have children. The children of their union are new creations. They would not exist except for the conscious choice of people.

Of course, animals can also participate in procreation. However, their offspring cannot change the world. Human beings, on the other hand, have the power to change the world. A decision to build a house, for example, is an idea that begins in the mind and later becomes objective reality. The fact that we have cars and roads to drive them on has only happened because a human had an idea. In the same way, planes, railroads, light bulbs, cell phones and computers are the result of humans visualizing a concept and then acting to make the concept a reality.

In a similar way, people are able to create their own future. If a person wants to be a barber or cosmetologist, he or she can go to a school and become what they want. Many, if not most, occupations today in America and much of the world are decided by choice. A teacher is a teacher and a doctor is a doctor only because each decided to devote a significant part of their lives to getting the necessary training.

The point is, we create much of our own world by the choices we make and the things we do to realize our objectives. In contrast, animals can do little to alter their environment. They live in nature as they find it and make only instinctual attempts to change their world for the better. They construct, for example, a bird nest or a beehive. There are no lasting monuments or literature left by animals. In contrast, the power of the human mind is phenomenal. Each of us has the capacity to make things happen. We have the power to create.

Not only do human beings create, we also give substance and value to things. An easy example is money. A $100 dollar bill is only paper. Intrinsically, it has almost no value. Similarly, the check we write or the small piece of plastic we swipe in a machine has no intrinsic value. Only because you, I, and others trust that it has value, does it have worth. The value is not in the small piece of paper or plastic, it is in our minds. True, it may be backed up by the government, but who is the government—it is other people.

Similarly, we assign value to things. Material things as well as people. Once our basic needs for food and shelter are met, we tend to think about other things we would like to have. People don't want everything; they dwell on the things they want most. They assign the highest value to them. Those things become our own particular desires, often quite different from the wants of others.

Throughout history, people have sought things to improve their lives. One major change has affected human beings in the last hundred years. Industrialists have found ways to make goods with machines, instead of having them made by hand. The machines make things quickly and cheaply. Consequently, today it is quite possible to become inundated with material objects.

The superabundance of material goods can affect our thinking as well as our lifestyle. People in industrial societies very often no longer live simply, but instead purchase all kinds of products and clothes to enhance their lifestyle. It is

interesting that old houses, built before the
twentieth century, seldom had closets. Only the
rich had them. Most people kept their few spare
clothes in a chest, often at the foot of the bed, and
those who were not rich often hung their "Sunday
best" garments on a hook on the wall.

Today, people contemplating buying a new
or newer house may not be satisfied with
traditional closets built into the side of a bedroom.
Instead, they often prefer walk-in closets to hold
all their garments. People today buy more clothes
than in the past because they are far cheaper than
when they were individually made by hand.

Part of the reason for buying more clothes
as well as other things is the reality of living in a
consumer world. Abetted by advertizing that is
pervasive in our society, it has become easy to
adopt a materialistic lifestyle.

How might this happen? Ads are
everywhere, on TV, the internet, on billboards, in
newspapers and magazines. Most are advising us
to make purchases. Often, the way advertisers
accomplish this is to tell us that if we are smart
we really <u>should</u> buy their product. They imply, or
sometimes deftly say that those who don't buy or
use their product are not smart, not beautiful, not
manly, not healthy, not up to date, or not
_____, you name it. Most people say they don't
pay attention to advertizing, but those who pay
for the ads know we do. They know that "name
recognition" alone can be significant when
choosing between two or more products.

Three major effects are likely from exposure to constant advertizing.

(1) People can easily become mentally preoccupied with themselves—their wants, their needs, their bodies, and their lack of what they see on television. It follows that self-esteem may be lowered. People may also spend much time thinking about how they can get the things they desire.

(2) Advertisers often employ those who represent authority figures. Although they are mostly actors, their body language and tone of voice represent people ad executives want us to listen to. Because authority figure are used to sell products, most of which we do not want or need, there may be a tendency to downplay those who speak with authority. Instead of listening to what such a person has to say, we may instead wonder, 'What is it that he or she trying to sell me.'

(3) The third follows from the first. Because we are sensitized by media to think mainly of our own material wants and needs, we may tend to spend little time thinking about the needs of others or of the spiritual dimension of our lives.

People are more than just matter—that is, only material bodies. Christians believe men and women are endowed with soul and spirit. Even atheists realize that people have consciousness, the unique human ability to remember the past and to make plans for the future.

Christ made it clear that our priorities should not be on the passing things of this life. His own words are: 'That is why I am telling you not to worry about your life and what you are to wear. Surely life is more than food, and the body more than clothing! Look at the birds in the sky. They do not sow or reap or gather into barns; yet your heavenly Father feeds them. Are you not worth much more than they are? Can any of you, however much you worry, add one single cubit to your span of life? And why worry about clothing? Think of the flowers growing in the fields; they never have to work or spin; yet I assure you that not even Solomon in all his royal robes was clothed like one of these. Now if that is how God clothes the wild flowers growing in the field which are there today and thrown into the furnace tomorrow, will he not much more look after you, you who have so little faith? So do not worry; do not say, "What are we to eat? What are we to drink? What are we to wear?" It is the gentiles who set their hearts on all these things. Your heavenly father knows you need them all. Set your hearts on his kingdom first, and on God's saving justice, and all these other things will be given to you as well. So do not worry about tomorrow: tomorrow will take care of itself. Each day has enough trouble of its own.' (Matt 6: 25-34)

Those who have small children know the great amount of care and love they need. Parents often forget themselves in caring for their children. Teenagers also need care, but of a different kind. They are able to do most things for themselves, but they need affirmation, direction, and most of all, love. Older people have lived long enough to feel they know what is important. Like others, they need people to care about them and they need to care about other people. For everyone, spontaneous or not so spontaneous acts of kindness toward others is the stuff of Christian living. Generosity and thankfulness for blessings is Christianity in action.

In order to do be able to do these things, time for reflection is important. Time to take a break from all the distractions is necessary for getting ones priorities in order. Without some time to tune out, it is easy to feel too busy and stressed. Psychologically, helping others is a great de-stressor. Time spent on the needs of others helps to put our own needs in perspective.

God knows we need time to be alone and to think. Christ himself did it often, leaving the apostles to go alone to pray. He recommends it. In Matthew, he was quite specific: "When you pray, go to your inner room, close the door, and pray to your Father in secret. And your Father who sees in secret will repay you. In praying, do not babble like the pagans, who think they will be heard because of their many words. Do not be like them. Your Father knows what you need before you ask him." (Matt 6: 6-8)

Sometimes, if we remember to listen, we may consciously be aware of God's answer to our prayer.

# Appendix III

## Christ and the Eucharist

We remember what Christ said at the last supper.

"Then he took the bread, and when he had given thanks, he broke it and gave it to them, saying, 'This is my body given for you; do this in remembrance of me.' He did the same with the cup after supper, and said, 'This cup is the new covenant in my blood poured out for you.' (Luke 22:19, 20)

Christ pointed to this moment before in his ministry. He told the Jews, "I am the bread of life. Your fathers ate manna in the desert and they are dead; but this is the bread which comes down from heaven, so that a person may eat it and not die. I am the living bread which has come down from heaven. Anyone who eats this bread will live for ever; and the bread that I shall give is my flesh, for the life of the world." (John 6: 48-51)

John's gospel shows that these words caused consternation in many of Christ's followers. Nevertheless, Christ continued even more forcefully to make clear to them what he was saying:

"In all truth I tell you, if you do not eat the flesh of the Son of man and drink his blood, you have no life in you. Anyone who does eat my flesh has eternal life, and I shall raise that person up on the last day. For my flesh is real food and my blood is real drink. Whoever eats my flesh and drinks my blood lives in me and I live in that person." (John 6:53-57)

Christ was aware of the effect his words were having on his followers. He knew that many would leave him. Those who left did not have the faith to wait and see how this could happen. Afterward, Christ turned to the twelve apostles, "What about you, do you want to go away too?" Peter answered for them all: "Lord, to whom shall we go? You have the message of eternal life, and we believe; we have come to know that you are the Holy One of God." (John 6: 68, 69)

With the Reformation in the sixteenth century, many of the Protestant churches abandoned belief in the real presence of Christ in the Eucharist. Other churches, including the

Catholic Church, Eastern Orthodox churches, and many Presbyterians and Lutheran Churches, etc. retain belief in the real changing of the bread and wine into Christ's body.

The miraculous change of ordinary bread and wine into Christ's body and blood is not something that can be seen. To all appearances, bread remains bread and wine remains wine. However, a scientifically minded person can recognize that the elements, the atoms, found in bread are the same kind of elements as those found in the human body. For God to change one to the other would not be difficult. However, for us it still takes faith.

Faith was lacking in those Jews who turned away when Christ said they should eat his flesh and drink his blood. Since Christ's institution of the Eucharist at the Last Supper, we have a better understanding of how we are enjoined to share in his life and Spirit. Some Christians turn away and say Communion has no meaning. Others believe they are only acting out the memory of Christ's last supper. For those who do believe, Christ's words come true. "Whoever eats my flesh and drinks my blood lives in me and I live in that person." (John 6:56) (See note 2)

# Discussion questions

## Chapter one

1. Why do you think Christ's disciples did not believe in his coming death?

2. Was it only the poor who followed Jesus? Explain.

3. What are some reasons why many of the Jews turned against Jesus?

## Chapter two

Who, what kind of men, took Jesus' body for burial?

Four different gospel writers tell of the Resurrection. What are some aspects of the Resurrection that are the same or similar for all?

Why do you think so many of Christ's disciples didn't recognize him after his resurrection?

Why didn't Jesus immediately tell the men traveling toward Emmaus who he was?

## Chapter three

What words did Christ use to institute the sacrament of Confession?

What is the old way and a newer way of receiving the sacrament of Penance?

What did it take for the apostle Thomas to believe in Christ's Resurrection?

## Chapter four

Who are the lambs and sheep that Christ talks about in this chapter?

Who do you think are the "other sheep. . .not of this fold" that Christ also wants to lead?

## Chapter five

Why do you think that at first Christ did not seem to want to help the Phoenician woman?

What is the "new message" that Christ emphasizes after his resurrection?

## Chapter six

The apostles didn't want Jesus to leave them.
Jesus told them ". . .it is better for you that I go."
Why did Christ tell them that?

Christ said he would <u>prepare</u> a place in heaven for
the apostles. Will he do the same for each of us?

## Chapter seven

Early Christians in Jerusalem didn't have a
church. Where did they meet?

What was Gamaliel's argument to the Sanhedrin
that saved the apostles?

How did the persecution of Christians in
Jerusalem lead to the spread of Christianity?

## Chapter eight

What are some traditional and not so traditional ways of receiving the Holy Spirit?

Why do you think Simon the magician was willing to pay for the powers of the Holy Spirit?

What are the gifts of the Holy Spirit?

The gifts of the Holy Spirit are opposed to the vices. What are the "works of the flesh" that Paul names?

What are the "fruits of the Spirit"?

Do you know someone who exemplifies the fruits of the Spirit in their lives? In what way?

How often should we ask, in a simple way, for the Spirit to come into our lives?

## Appendix I

What are some of the main differences between Christian and atheistic beliefs?

Even today, with modern laboratories, scientists cannot create life. Do you think that somehow it could have started on its own long ago?

## Appendix II

At first glance, do you tend to think of tragedies, sudden deaths, etc as the work of God or of nature?

What is the "Big Bang Theory", and what role might God have in it?

Why, in the solar system, is the earth in a particularly good place?

What are some of the many ways people are different from apes and animals?

Do you personally pay any attention to advertizing?

How might advertizing make us focus on material needs rather than spiritual needs?

What is Christ's answer for getting our priorities in order?

# Prayers to the Holy Spirit

There are prayers specifically addressed to the Holy Spirit, or ask God to send the Spirit. As Christ said, "If you then, who are wicked, know how to give good gifts to your children, how much more will the Father in heaven give the Holy Spirit to those who ask him?" (Luke 11: 13) A few of these prayers are listed below.

**Come Holy Spirit**, fill the hearts of your faithful and enkindle in them the fire of your love. Send forth your Spirit and they shall be created. And You shall renew the face of the earth.

Oh, God, who by the light of the Holy Spirit, did instruct the hearts of the faithful, grant that by the same Holy Spirit we may be truly wise, and ever enjoy His consolations, through Christ Our Lord, amen.

## Prayer for the Indwelling of the Spirit
St. Augustine, est. about 390 AD

Holy Spirit, powerful Consoler, Sacred Bond of the Father and the Son, Hope of the afflicted, descend into my heart and establish in it your loving dominion. Enkindle in my tepid soul the fire of your love so that I may be wholly subject to you. We believe that when you dwell in us, you also prepare a dwelling for the Father and the Son. Deign, therefore, to come to me, Consoler of abandoned souls, and Protector of the needy. Help the afflicted, strengthen the weak, and support the wavering. Come and purify me. Let no evil desire take possession of me. You love the humble and resist the proud. Come to me, glory of the living, and hope of the dying. Lead me by your grace that I may always be pleasing to you. Amen.

## Prayer for the help of the Holy Spirit
St. Anthony of Padua, est. about 1225AD

O God, send forth your Holy Spirit into my heart that I may perceive, and into my soul that I may meditate. Inspire me to speak with piety, holiness, tenderness and mercy. Teach, guide and direct my thoughts and senses from beginning to end. May your grace ever help and correct me, and may I be strengthened now with wisdom from on high, for the sake of your infinite mercy. Amen.

## A prayer to the Holy Spirit
Modern, anonymous

Spirit of wisdom and understanding, enlighten our minds to perceive the mysteries of the universe in relation to eternity. Spirit of right judgment and courage, guide us and make us firm in our baptismal decision to follow Jesus' way of love. Spirit of knowledge and reverence, help us to see the lasting value of justice and mercy in our everyday dealings with one another. May we respect life as we work to solve problems of family and nation, economy and ecology. Spirit of God, spark our faith, hope and love into new action each day. Fill our lives with wonder and awe in your presence which penetrates all creation.

## Glory be

Glory to the Father, the Son, and the Holy Spirit. As it was in the beginning, is now and ever shall be, world without end. Amen.

## About the author

Tom Molnar is an author of fiction as well as short works on religious themes. As for the latter, early on he questioned his faith. His search for answers in history, science and scripture has led him to the understanding that God is real, caring, and the One who makes everything possible.

Tom is not a trained theologian. He does not have the official answers a doctor of the church might have. An electronic technician in the US Army, degreed in sociology with a major concentration in history, most of his experience has been working with people as an employment counselor, office manager, and veteran representative, while raising four children with his wife, Kathleen.

As a creative writer of fiction, he is grateful his nonfiction relating to religious themes has received the approval of priests, nuns, and the local bishop.

More than anything, Tom enjoys telling a good story, whether fictional or true-to-life. .

Books you might like by Tom Molnar

# A Quick Look at Heaven

## And Hell

A view unlike any we might imagine

Amazon, $2.99

Few know what heaven will be like, yet most of us hope to go there. Misconceptions abound, making it hard to know what to expect. Some common views of eternity are disturbing for those who are actively involved in the bustle and satisfactions of life.

Fortunately, many of the old notions can now be laid to rest. Drawing from scriptural passages, scientific advances, and life after death experiences, we can come to grips with a heaven that is both exciting and fulfilling.

"I congratulate you on this book. May this Year of Faith be a time of special grace for you."

Bishop Dale J. Melczek

# Dark Age Maiden

Since the tragedy that destroyed his family, Uberto has lived by his sword and his wits. He wants full knighthood and the hand of the not easily won Lady Carina. Two things stand in his way: a renowned sword fighter, Count Giancarlo, and the Muslim invasion of France.

Lady Carina has thoughts of her own. She has boldly turned down her father's choice for marriage. Now, she finds herself sought by a gallant knight and a wealthy count. Before long, she comes to know the power of love. But is it too late?

## Historical fiction, laced with love

Amazon, Barnes & Noble

$2.99 download edition   $8.99 paperback

(Also reviewed in Catholic Fiction.net)

# Mary, the Girl who said Yes

When Mary said yes, she didn't know how her answer would change her life. She didn't know her son would be born in a shelter for animals, or that she would have to flee a murderous king who sought to kill her child. Nor did she know that her son's life on earth would be far from glorious.

Mary's story is one of danger and excitement, love, sorrow and uncertainty. She had to be strong to face the trials that would come. Delving into her life as seen in the Gospels shows a spirited and courageous woman, a fitting mother for Jesus, the man of God who changed history.

"A good overview of Mary and the times she lived in. Very nicely done." Rev. Joseph Hannon S.D.B., St. Petersburg, Florida.

"I very much enjoyed your reflections on Mary," Bishop Dale Melczek.

"An interesting story told in a clever manner." Suzy Watts, book reviewer.

Amazon

# Tara's World

## A Land of Beauty, Danger, and Love

A girl appeared at the edge of the secluded pond. She stepped into the water, wading to the deep. Beautiful, she turned toward him. . .

Tara has never before  met a man like Nick. She is drawn to him, yet there is something about him she does not understand. Is it a trait of all humans?

Nick and Tara have much to learn about each other as they fight to remain in this beautiful new world filled with danger.

Formerly *"Bridestar"*

"Bridestar [*Tara's World*] is the true standout star...lively and exciting. Its subtle alien nature is just exotic enough to tantalize a reader with the possibilities."
–Heartstrings reviews

"I will definitely be watching for the sequels to [*Tara's World*] –Book Review Cafe

On Amazon,  download, $2.99  paperback $9.99

# Christianity, the Challenge of a Changing World

Is worldwide Christianity in decline, or is it changing and growing?

How are men and women personally affected by the new culture?

Have the advances of the twentieth century reduced the need for faith?

Has religious belief been transformed by the popular ideas of Darwin, Freud, Hugh Hefner and others?

Does Christ continue to make a difference in the modern world? In what way?

Tom Molnar looks at the impact of our rapidly changing culture on our lives and on Christianity. A well researched, easy to read book with some surprising findings. Includes *A Quick Look at Heaven*.

Amazon, Barnes & Noble

# Notes

1. Most Christian religions believe that angels are spiritual beings (without bodies) who are far superior in intellect to human beings. They too, were permitted to accept God or reject Him. Those who turned away from God are the "fallen angels" known to us as devils. Because the angels are super intelligent beings, their choice not to serve is irrevocable.

2. In specifically Catholic teaching, only a priest during the Mass can change, "transubstantiate" is the term used, the bread and wine into Christ's body and blood. Many other Christian faiths believe in the "real presence" of Christ in the Eucharist though not specifically in "transubstantiation."